THE RISE OF EVOLVED SPECIES

A Guide
to the Next Generation of
Life Forms
in a Changing World

By

Zhenbo Lu

TABLE OF CONTENTS

Preface

The world is changing rapidly, and so is the life on this planet. As human beings continue to advance and develop, we have inadvertently impacted the environment, causing changes that have profound effects on the Earth's ecosystems. These changes can lead to the evolution of new species, whether they be animals, plants, or microorganisms.

This book, aims to introduce these new species to young readers. With exquisite illustrations, this book is suitable for children aged 8+, and it not only introduces basic biological knowledge but also helps children realize the impact of human beings on the environment and the importance of environmental protection.

Although it's difficult to predict exactly what kind of creatures will evolve in the future, it's safe to say that the impact of human development on the environment will play a significant role in shaping the evolution of life on Earth. This book introduces 20 hypothetical examples of organisms that might evolve as a result of human impact on the environment. This book makes reasonable speculations and assumptions about the future species changes that may be caused by the impact of human development on the ecological environment. It aims to arouse people's awareness of environmental protection, popularize biological science knowledge.

In the past few years, we have experienced a global pandemic caused by a new coronavirus. This pandemic has brought significant changes to the world, forcing us to rethink our relationship with the environment and other living beings. It has also highlighted the need for us to be more mindful of the impact we have on the planet and to work towards a sustainable future.

As we look to the future, we must consider how our actions will impact the evolution of life on this planet. We must learn to balance our development with environmental protection and strive to create a world where we can coexist with other living beings. This book aims to inspire children to think about the world around them and to imagine the possibilities that lie ahead.

In the following pages, you will meet some fascinating new species that have evolved due to human impact on the environment. You will learn about their unique characteristics, habitats, and how they have adapted to survive in a changing world. It is our hope that this book will not only educate but also inspire young readers to take action and become stewards of the environment.

Let us embark on this journey of discovery together, and let us remember that we all have a role to play in creating a sustainable future for ourselves and the planet we call home.

I

ANIMALS

Photovore Bugs

A unique and fascinating species that is unlike any other insect you've ever seen! These bugs boast an appearance that sets them apart from their peers. Their reflective or iridescent exoskeletons are not just for show, but actually help them collect and absorb light energy. With specialized appendages or organs that can convert light into food, these bugs truly have a light-based metabolism.

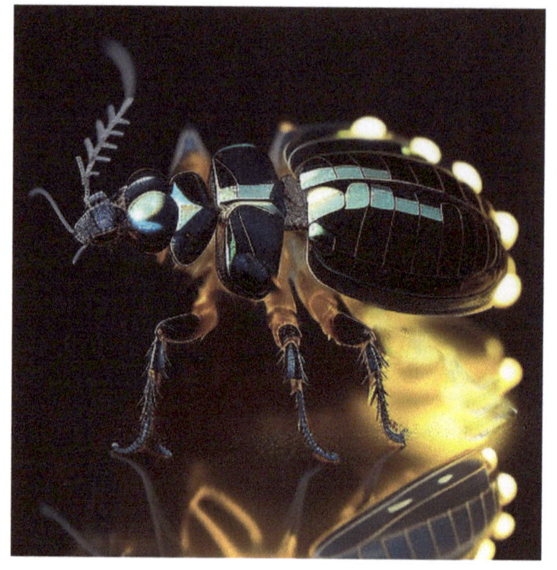

To survive in harsh and polluted environments, Photovore bugs have evolved to have black exoskeletons that are highly reflective. They also have large, flat antennae that can collect light from multiple angles, enabling them to gather enough energy to survive in environments contaminated by industrial pollution. This unique adaptation is crucial, as they can tolerate high levels of pollution and contaminants that would be toxic to other organisms.

Their presence in such areas is important as they help to clean up pollution by converting it into food energy. As they play a critical role in maintaining the balance of ecosystems and keeping the planet healthy, understanding their features and the role they play is crucial.

Characteristics:

- Light-based metabolism: Photovore bugs feed on light energy, and have evolved specialized systems that allow them to convert light into food.
- Tolerance to pollution: These bugs are able to tolerate high levels of pollution and contaminants, and can survive in environments that would be toxic to other organisms.
- Reflective or iridescent exoskeletons: The reflective or iridescent exoskeletons of photovore bugs help to increase their ability to collect and absorb light energy.
- Specialized appendages or organs: Photovore bugs may have specialized appendages or organs that allow them to convert light energy into food.

Evolutionary Reason:

One such adaptation is the development of photovore bugs. In order to survive in contaminated environments, these bugs have evolved to feed on light energy. This unique method of metabolism allows them to bypass the polluted food sources that other organisms rely on, such as plants or other insects. Photovore bugs are able to collect and absorb light energy through their reflective or iridescent exoskeletons, which have evolved to be highly efficient at gathering light energy. They also have specialized systems, such as large flat antennae, that can collect light from multiple angles.

It is important to note that the evolutionary process is not intentional, and photovore bugs did not evolve with the specific purpose of cleaning up pollution. Rather, their ability to survive in contaminated environments and feed on light energy has given them an advantage over other organisms, which has allowed them to thrive in these areas.

Overall, the evolution of photovore bugs is a fascinating example of how organisms can adapt and evolve in response to human impact on the environment. By understanding the evolutionary reasons behind the development of these unique species, we can gain insight into how other organisms may adapt and evolve in the future as human activity continues to impact the natural world.

Aquatic Filter Fish

Aquatic filter fish may have a variety of appearances, depending on the species. However, they may have specialized structures, such as gills or fins, that help to filter contaminants from the water.

These fish would have specialized gills that allow them to filter heavy metals and pollutants from the water. They may have a slightly translucent appearance, allowing them to blend in with the water and avoid predators. Additionally, they may have a filter system within their bodies that helps to process the pollutants they filter from the water.

Characteristics:

- Heavy metal and pollutant filtration: Aquatic filter fish are able to filter heavy metals and pollutants from contaminated waters, making them a valuable species in efforts to clean up polluted areas.
- Specialized gills or fins: These fish may have specialized gills or fins that help to filter contaminants from the water.
- Tolerance to high levels of pollutants: Aquatic filter fish are able to tolerate high levels of pollutants, making them well suited to survive in contaminated environments.
- Bioaccumulation: These fish may also accumulate high levels of pollutants in their bodies, which can be harmful to their health. However, they play a critical role in helping to remove pollutants from the environment.

The presence of aquatic filter fish in contaminated areas is important because they help to clean up the water, removing pollutants and heavy metals that would otherwise be harmful to other species. However, this fish accumulate a lot of heavy metals and toxins, so it cannot be treated as a food source.

Evolutionary Reason:

The residues of chemical fertilizers and pesticides used in agriculture will flow into the rivers and lakes with rainwater or groundwater, and the wastewater discharged from industrial production will cause serious pollution to the river. In this case, it becomes difficult for ordinary fish to survive. The emergence of this fish is precisely due to the evolution of the ability to adapt to highly polluted water bodies, and can purify water bodies to a certain extent.

Ground-Dwelling Lizards

Ground-Dwelling Lizards have undergone a fascinating evolutionary transformation to survive in the concrete jungle of urban areas. These lizards possess a streamlined appearance that allows them to dart quickly through the urban landscape, with specialized structures on their feet that enable them to grip onto hard surfaces with ease.

To blend in with their urban surroundings, these lizards may have evolved a camouflage coloring that mirrors the concrete and asphalt. They may also be smaller in size than their rural counterparts, as they have adapted to limited spaces and can easily hide in crevices and small openings. Their strong legs and tail allow them to climb walls and buildings to escape danger, and they have become more omnivorous, feeding on insects, flowers, and small seeds found in urban areas.

In addition to these physical adaptations, ground-dwelling lizards may also possess enhanced hearing and vision to detect predators, food, and potential mates more efficiently. These are just a few examples of the many fascinating changes these lizards may have undergone to survive in urban areas.

Evolutionary reason:

Ground-dwelling lizards have likely evolved to live in densely populated urban areas due to the destruction of natural habitats and the growth of urban areas. As cities continue to expand and natural habitats are destroyed, these lizards have been forced to adapt to survive in a more urbanized environment. Ground-dwelling lizards may have once lived in rural areas, but the increasing urbanization and fragmentation of their natural habitat has made it difficult for them to survive. In order to survive in urban environments, these lizards may have developed a variety of adaptations, such as a smaller size and a more omnivorous diet that allows them to feed on the small insects, flowers, and seeds found in cities. They may have also developed stronger legs and tails to climb walls and buildings, and better hearing and vision to detect predators and prey in crowded environments.

Furthermore, ground-dwelling lizards are able to take advantage of the resources provided by urbanization, such as warm surfaces like concrete and asphalt, which they can use to regulate their body temperature. They can also find refuge in small crevices and openings in buildings, which can provide protection from predators and other environmental stressors. As a result of these adaptations, ground-dwelling lizards are able to survive and even thrive in densely populated urban environments, making them an important part of the ecosystem in these areas.

Air-Purifying Moths

Air-purifying moths are fascinating creatures that have evolved to detect and feed on air pollutants, such as microscopic particles and chemical compounds. These moths may have distinguishing features, such as a specialized proboscis or dense hair-like structures, which allow them to better absorb air pollutants. They are often found in areas with high levels of air pollution, such as cities or industrial sites, and could play an important role in maintaining the health of the air and the overall environment. In addition, their vibrant and colorful appearance make them a beautiful sight to behold in urban environments.

One of the most remarkable characteristics of air-purifying moths is their ability to feed on air pollutants. They have evolved to consume particulate matter and other harmful substances found in the air, making them a valuable tool in efforts to clean up polluted urban environments. These moths have a strong sense of smell and are able to locate and consume pollutants with ease. They are also highly resistant to the toxic effects of air pollutants, making them well-suited for life in contaminated environments.

Air-purifying moths are typically small in size, with soft, delicate wings and a bright, vibrant coloration that helps them to stand out in their urban habitats. Their unique appearance and ability to purify the air make them an important part of the ecosystem in densely populated areas, helping to ensure that the air is clean and healthy for all residents.

Evolutionary reason:

Air pollution is a growing problem in many highly populated areas, with harmful pollutants such as nitrogen oxides, sulfur dioxide, and particulate matter becoming increasingly common. The negative impact of air pollution on human health and the environment is well documented, and efforts are being made to reduce and eliminate these pollutants. In this environment, air-purifying moths have evolved to consume these pollutants, providing a natural and effective way to mitigate the harmful effects of air pollution.

As air pollution has become more prevalent, these moths have adapted to their environment by developing specialized organs and senses that allow them to locate and feed on airborne pollutants. Over time, the moths have become highly resistant to the toxic effects of these pollutants, allowing them to thrive in contaminated environments that would be inhospitable to other organisms.

The ability of these moths to consume and process pollutants makes them a valuable addition to the ecosystem in highly populated areas. By consuming pollutants, they help to clean the air and reduce the negative impact of air pollution on human health and the environment. This adaptation is an important example of nature's ability to evolve in response to changing environmental conditions and highlights the importance of preserving biodiversity and protecting natural habitats.

Magnetoreceptive Birds

Imagine a bird with shimmering, iridescent feathers that change color in the light. This is the Magnetoreceptive bird, a future animal that has evolved with a unique biological compass that allows them to navigate using the Earth's magnetic field. The bird may look similar in appearance to other bird species, but its tiny iron mineral particles in its beaks act as a biological compass, allowing it to sense the Earth's magnetic field and orient itself during migration.

Magnetoreceptive birds are known for their incredible navigation abilities, which allow them to undertake long-distance migrations with impressive accuracy. They are able to detect changes in the Earth's magnetic field and use this information to navigate across vast distances, even in the absence of landmarks or other visual cues. In addition, research has shown that magnetoreceptive birds have a range of other fascinating abilities, including the ability to perceive and respond to polarized light, as well as the ability to detect and respond to subtle changes in air pressure.

Magnetoreceptive birds are known for their incredible navigation abilities, which allow them to undertake long-distance migrations with impressive accuracy. In fact, they can detect changes in the Earth's magnetic field and use this information to navigate across vast distances, even in the absence of landmarks or other visual cues. And that's not all! These birds have a range of other fascinating abilities, such as the ability to perceive and respond to polarized light, as well as the ability to detect and respond to subtle changes in air pressure.

Evolutionary reason:

Magnetoreceptive birds have evolved their unique biological compass as a way to aid their long-distance migrations. During migration, birds face numerous environmental challenges such as unpredictable weather conditions and scarce food resources. Navigating using the Earth's magnetic field allows birds to take the most direct route to their destination and avoid obstacles such as mountains and bodies of water. This ability to navigate using the Earth's magnetic field is especially important during nocturnal migrations or when visual cues are limited, such as during cloudy or foggy weather.

However, magnetoreceptive birds' evolution may also be linked to environmental changes caused by human activity. Air pollution and the rapid changes to landscapes can make traditional means of navigation difficult for birds. The ability to detect the Earth's magnetic field provides a backup method for birds to navigate over long distances, allowing them to adapt to these changing environmental conditions. In addition, the increased electromagnetic radiation in the environment from technology may interfere with birds' natural navigation abilities, further driving the evolution of magnetoreceptive birds. Ultimately, the evolution of magnetoreceptive birds is a fascinating example of how animals can adapt and evolve in response to changing environmental conditions, both natural and human-made.

Acid-resistant shellfish

Acid-tolerant marine shellfish refer to shellfish molluscs that can survive and reproduce in a marine environment with high acidity. As pollution levels increase, there is more sulfur dioxide, carbon dioxide dissolved in the water, which can lead to increased ocean acidification, making it harder for native shellfish to survive. However, some of them have developed adaptations that allow them to tolerate these changing conditions.

The appearance of acid-resistant marine shellfish varies widely. Most shellfish have an acid-resistant outer layer that protects their shell or exoskeleton from acid, and their internal anatomy may change to help regulate the acidity of their body fluids.

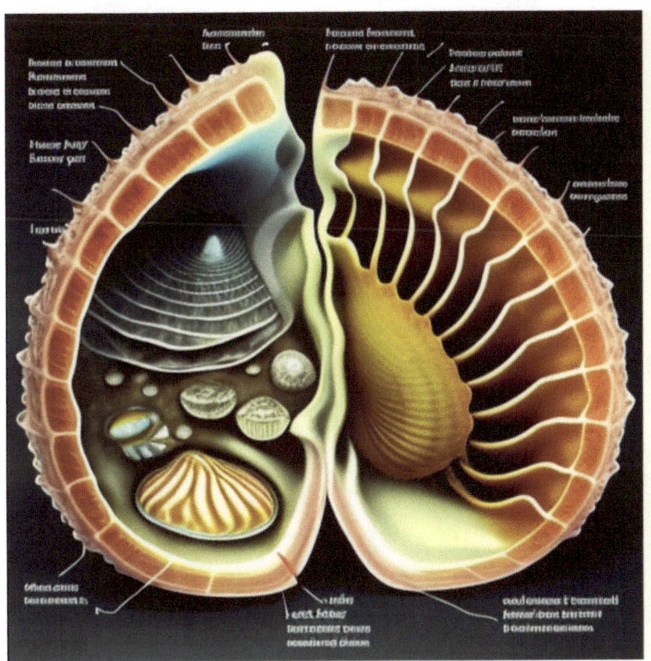
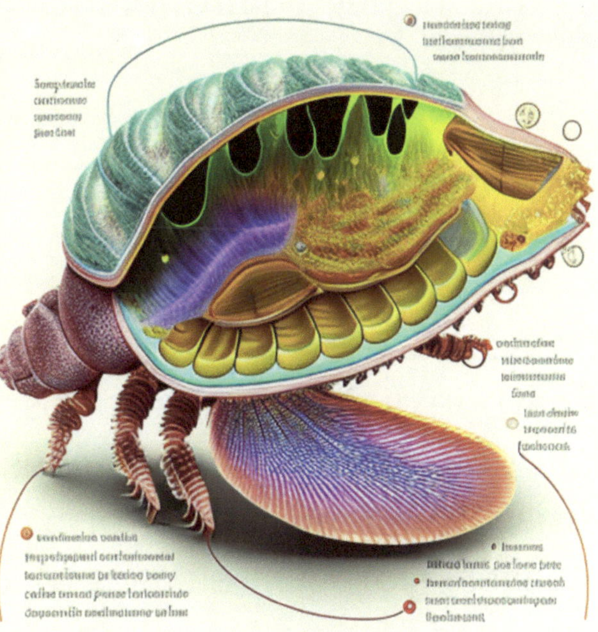

Some of chacteristics:

- Tolerance to low pH: Those animals with exoskeletons have developed a mucus layer to protect their internal calcium carbonate components from acid, allowing them to thrive in acidic oceans.
- Ability to absorb and neutralize excess acid: Some acid-tolerant species have adaptations, such as changes in internal anatomy or the presence of specific enzymes, that help them absorb and neutralize excess acid in their environment.

Evolutionary reason:

The oceans are becoming more acidic due to increasing levels of carbon dioxide in the atmosphere, as well as industrial pollution. As carbon dioxide dissolves in seawater, it reacts with water molecules to form carbonic acid, which in turn releases hydrogen releases to, decrease in pH levels and increased acidity. This phenomenon is known as ocean acidification.

In response to this changing environment, acid-resistant shellfish may have evolved to survive and thrive in increasingly acidic oceans. These organisms have developed various adaptations to tolerate low pH levels, such as the ability to produce a slime layer on calcium intercalate Components from acid, or changes to their internal anatomy that help them to absorb and neutralize excess acid in their environment.

Overall, the emergence of acid-resistant shellfish is an example of evolutionary adaptation in response to changing environmental conditions, highlighting the remarkable ability of organisms to adapt and thrive in the face of environmental challenges.

UV-Resistant Insects

Imagine walking through a park on a sunny day and seeing swarms of insects gathering on tree trunks. Those are the UV-resistant insects, shimmering in the sunlight and impervious to its harmful radiation. These insects have evolved with features such as darker pigmentation, thicker cuticles, or special pigments that protect them from the sun's ultraviolet light.

UV-resistant insects are unique in their ability to tolerate higher levels of UV radiation than other insects. Their appearance can vary, but they all have one thing in common: they are survivors. Some have darker pigmentation, which helps them absorb and scatter UV radiation, while others have thicker cuticles that provide a physical barrier between their bodies and their environment. Some even have special pigments, such as melanin, that absorb and neutralize UV radiation.

Characteristics:

- Tolerance to UV radiation: UV resistant insects are able to tolerate higher levels of UV radiation than other insects, allowing them to continue to thrive in their environment.
- Darker pigmentation: Some UV-resistant insects may have darker pigmentation that helps absorb and scatter UV radiation, thus protecting them from harmful effects.
- Thicker cuticles: Other UV-resistant insects may have thicker cuticles that provide a physical barrier between their bodies and their environment and help block UV radiation.
- Special Pigments: Some insects may have special pigments, such as melanin, that absorb and neutralize UV radiation, protecting the insect from its harmful effects.

Evolutionary reason:

UV-resistant insects have evolved as a response to the increasing levels of ultraviolet radiation caused by the destruction of the ozone layer, which has been primarily caused by human activities such as the use of chlorofluorocarbons (CFCs) and other ozone-depleting substances.

As the ozone layer is depleted, the amount of harmful UV radiation reaching the Earth's surface increases, making it difficult for some insects to survive. Insects that are able to withstand higher levels of UV radiation have an advantage in these changing environments. Over time, natural selection favors these UV-resistant traits, allowing these insects to thrive and continue to pass on their advantageous traits to future generations. As UV radiation levels continue to increase, the variety and number of UV-resistant insects will increase.

Water-Collecting Beetles

Imagine living in an environment where water is a scarce resource. That's the harsh reality for Water-Collecting Beetles, a fascinating type of beetle that has evolved to survive in some of the driest and hottest regions on Earth. These small beetles have a range of unique adaptations that help them to collect and store water, ensuring their survival in an otherwise inhospitable environment.

At first glance, Water-Collecting Beetles might seem like any other beetle with a shiny exoskeleton, but upon closer inspection, their unique features become apparent. These beetles are relatively small, measuring only a few centimeters in length, but they have a streamlined, oval-shaped body that allows them to move quickly across hot, dry surfaces.

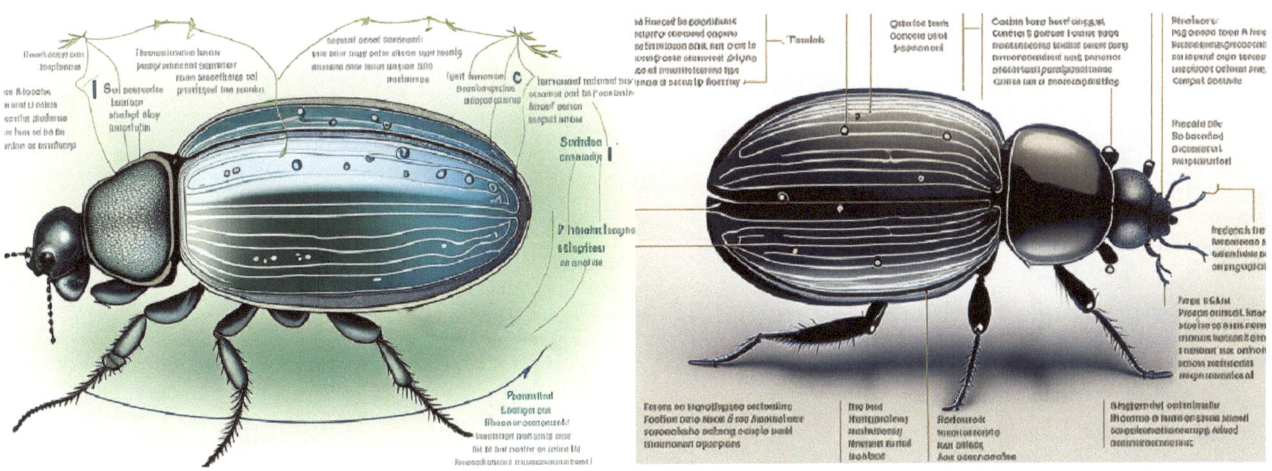

What sets Water-Collecting Beetles apart is their ability to collect and store water in their bodies. They have specialized grooves on their backs that channel water towards their mouthparts, where it is collected and stored in a specialized cavity. This water is then used by the beetle for drinking or other important functions, like regulating body temperature.

But that's not all. Water-Collecting Beetles also have other adaptations that help them conserve water. For example, they are able to close their spiracles, tiny holes on their bodies used for breathing, to reduce water loss. They can also enter a state of suspended animation during periods of drought, conserving energy and water until conditions improve.

It's incredible to think about the adaptations that Water-Collecting Beetles have developed over time to survive in some of the harshest environments on Earth. From their unique grooves to their ability to enter a state of suspended animation, these small beetles have mastered the art of water collection and conservation.

Water-collecting beetles are a fascinating example of how organisms can adapt to their environment in order to survive. It is believed that these beetles may have evolved their unique ability to collect and store water in response to changing environmental conditions. In many arid regions, water scarcity is a major challenge for both plants and animals, and the destruction of vegetation due to deforestation and other human activities can exacerbate this problem. In such environments, water-collecting beetles are able to thrive by using their specialized grooves to collect and store water from even the smallest sources. By evolving this ability, these beetles are able to gain a competitive advantage over other insects and survive in habitats where water is scarce. This adaptation not only helps them to survive in harsh conditions, but also ensures that they are able to carry on their species, ultimately contributing to the balance of the ecosystem.

Wind-Powered Insects

Wind-Powered Insects are one of nature's most incredible creations. Their streamlined bodies and elongated wings allow them to fly effortlessly through the air, even in the most challenging conditions. These insects have developed an incredible ability to harness the power of the wind, which has given them a distinct advantage over other species.

In addition to their efficient design, Wind-Powered Insects also have specialized sensors that allow them to detect changes in wind direction and adjust their flight path accordingly. These sensors are so advanced that they can even detect changes in wind speed and adjust their wing movements to maximize lift and minimize drag.

One of the most remarkable things about Wind-Powered Insects is their ability to travel great distances in search of food and water. They are able to fly at incredible speeds, and can cover hundreds of miles in a single day. This makes them ideal for exploring new habitats and finding sources of food and water that other insects cannot reach.

Another important role that Wind-Powered Insects may play is in pollination. Their ability to fly long distances and reach flowers that other insects cannot access makes them ideal pollinators. They are able to transport pollen from one flower to another, which helps to ensure the continued survival of many plant species.

The evolution of Wind-Powered Insects is a testament to the incredible adaptability of nature. As environmental conditions change, species must adapt or face extinction. Wind-Powered Insects have adapted in a remarkable way, allowing them to thrive in windy environments and play an important role in the ecosystem.

Evolutionary reason:

As humans continue to alter the natural landscape, many insect species are struggling to find food and resources in their changing environment. This has forced them to adapt in unique ways to survive. One such adaptation is the development of wind-powered abilities. Insects that can harness the energy of the wind are able to move across vast distances with less energy expenditure than those that rely solely on their own power.

The evolution of wind-powered insects may have been a response to the increasing difficulty of finding food and water in certain environments. By relying on the wind for travel, these insects are able to cover more ground and explore new habitats without exhausting their energy reserves. This not only helps them find food and water sources but also reduces their exposure to predators and other risks that come with long-distance travel.

In conclusion, the evolution of wind-powered insects is a remarkable example of adaptation to changing environmental conditions. By harnessing the power of the wind, these insects are able to conserve energy, travel more efficiently, and explore new habitats. Their unique abilities have helped them to survive and thrive in an ever-changing world.

II
PLANTS

Salt-tolerant Plant

Salt-tolerant plants are a fascinating example of plant evolution and hold great potential for various applications in the future. They can be used to rehabilitate degraded lands, improve soil quality, and increase food security in areas where water resources are scarce.

One of the most interesting salt-tolerant plants is Saltbush. This plant has small, waxy leaves that are adapted to prevent water loss, and are covered in salt crystals that are excreted from the plant. The salt crystals protect the plant from excessive salt accumulation, while the waxy leaves help to prevent water loss in the arid climate. In addition to its unique adaptations, Saltbush can be used in land rehabilitation projects to prevent soil erosion and improve soil structure.

Another fascinating salt-tolerant plant is salt orchid. It is a grass species that is commonly found along the coasts and in wetlands. It has long, narrow leaves that are adapted to tolerate saltwater, and the plant's roots are capable of excreting excess salt from the soil. This allows the plant to grow in highly saline soils where other plants cannot survive. Salt orchid has shown potential for use in golf courses and other sports fields due to its ability to tolerate saltwater irrigation. This could reduce the reliance on freshwater resources for irrigation and provide a more sustainable option for maintaining these fields.

Salt-tolerant crops have immense potential to address global food security challenges. By cultivating crops that can grow in saline soils, we can expand agricultural production in regions where fresh water resources are limited, and food scarcity is a major issue. This could improve the livelihoods of millions of people around the world and contribute to sustainable development. Some examples of salt-tolerant crops include barley, rice, wheat, and maize, which have been artificially cultivated to solve the issue of food security in regions where water resources are limited.

Due to the discharge of industrial pollution, rising sea levels, overuse of irrigation, the reduction of available fresh water and the excessive use of chemical fertilizers, the soil is gradually salinized, and some plants have evolved to adapt to high-salt soil. Their unique adaptations allow them to thrive in environments where other plants cannot survive.

Salt-tolerant crops have been artificially cultivated to solve the issue of food security in regions where water resources are limited.

Evolutionary reason:

The evolution of salt-tolerant plants is not only necessary but also urgent due to the increasing soil salinization caused by human activities. Industrial pollution, rising sea levels, overuse of irrigation, and the excessive use of chemical fertilizers are major contributors to soil salinization. As a result, some plants have evolved to adapt to high-salt soil.

The potential benefits of salt-tolerant plants are enormous, ranging from food security to environmental protection. The study of these species can provide valuable insights into plant evolution and help us develop new strategies to address global challenges. In a world where water resources are becoming increasingly scarce, salt-tolerant plants offer a glimmer of hope for a sustainable future. So, artificial assisted evolution provides another possibility

Thermal-Tolerant Plant

Climate change is rapidly altering the world we live in, with rising temperatures and erratic weather patterns causing widespread damage to ecosystems and threatening the survival of many species. However, amidst these challenges, there are also remarkable examples of nature's resilience and ada One such resilience. An example is the emergence of thermal-tolerant plants, a group of plants that have evolved to thrive in the face of extreme heat and drought.

Thermal-tolerant plants have a unique set of characteristics that enable them to survive in hot and arid environments. For instance, some species have small leaves with a reflective coating that can withstand temperatures of 40-80 °C in the sun, while others have a deep root system that can access water and nutrients from deep below the soil surface.

Additionally, some thermal-tolerant plants have specialized structures that help to regulate their internal temperature, allowing them to survive in hot environments.

These plants are not only vital for their ability to survive in a changing climate, but they also play a crucial role in maintaining biodiversity and ecosystem health. With habitats changing rapidly, many species are struggling to adapt, but thermal-tolerant plants a can prov Home and food sources for other species that would otherwise struggle to survive.

The appearance of thermal-tolerant plants is incredibly diverse, with each species having its unique adaptations that help them to conserve moisture and withstand high temperatures. Some species have thicker cuticles or small leaves that reduce moisture loss, while that others have specialized tissue . These adaptations provide a glimpse into the remarkable ways in which nature can adapt and evolve to changing conditions.

Evolutionary reason:

The evolution of thermal-tolerant plants is a fascinating and complex topic that involves natural selection, genetic variation, and environmental pressures. As the Earth's climate has changed over time, plants have had to adapt to new conditions to survive. Tolerant plants are likely due to a combination of these factors, with those individuals better adapted to hot and arid conditions more likely to survive and pass on their genes to future generations.

One of the most exciting things about thermal-tolerant plants is their potential for agriculture. With the increasing threat of climate change, it is becoming more and more difficult to grow crops in many areas of the world. However, by using thermal-tolerant plants , we may be able to develop new crops that can withstand extreme heat and drought conditions. This could help to ensure food security for millions of people around the world.

In conclusion, thermal-tolerant plants are a remarkable example of nature's ability to adapt and evolve in the face of a changing climate. They provide hope for the future and offer us new opportunities to sustainably grow crops and protect biodiversity. By studying these plants and Taking action to address climate change, we can work towards a brighter and more resilient future for ourselves and for the natural world.

Fish-eating plant

Aquatic plants have always been a fascinating subject for scientists and nature enthusiasts alike. The beauty and diversity of underwater flora are often stunning, but there is one particular plant that takes this fascination to a whole new level: the piscivorous plant, also known as the fish-eating plant.

Imagine a plant that not only grows in water but also eats fish! This unique plant is a seagrass-shaped aquatic plant that obtains the extra nutrients it needs to grow by hunting fish and other small aquatic animals. As predators in the water, their hunting ability is by no means inferior.

The plant may be tall, with long, thin leaves shaped like a web with fine edges to allow water to pass through. The leaves are covered with small, sticky glands that attract small aquatic animals, including fish. Once caught, the glands secrete digestive enzymes that break down the prey into plant-usable nutrients.

Piscivorous plants have evolved a number of specialized traits to become efficient hunters. First, the plant has long, thin stems with sharp, curved spines protruding from the surface. These spines are covered with a sticky slimy substance that helps the plant grab and hold its prey.

When the fish swims near the plant, the spines sense movement in the water and start moving, like the tendrils of a sea anemone. The spines wrap around the fish and hold it in place, while the sticky mucus helps prevent the fish from escaping.

As the fish struggles to break free, the plant begins to secrete digestive enzymes that break down the fish flesh, allowing the plants to absorb nutrients. Over time, the fish is completely digested, leaving only some small bones and other inedible parts.

Evolutionary reason:

The reason why aquatic plants and fish cannot directly obtain nutrients from the soil or water is mainly due to the lack of sufficient nutrients, such as nitrogen and phosphorus, in their growth environments. These elements are crucial for the healthy growth and reproduction of plants, but are difficult to obtain in the water where these plants grow. Compared to plants on land, the growth environment of aquatic plants is more complex and challenging because they need to absorb nutrients in water and are often subject to the impact of water flow and waves. This requires aquatic plants to evolve some special physiological and morphological features to adapt to this environment and help them survive and reproduce.

To cope with this environment, aquatic plants have evolved a special way of obtaining these essential nutrients: by preying on small aquatic animals to absorb these nutrients. This special way of nutrient intake allows these plants to survive and reproduce in water and become an important part of the top food chain in aquatic ecosystems.

Fire-Resistant Trees

The world is changing, and the fires that once swept through forests only once a century are now a common occurrence. Climate change and land-use practices have resulted in an increase in the frequency and intensity of wildfires, leaving a trail of destruction in their wake. But amidst the chaos, a ray of hope shines through - fire-resistant trees.

Fire-resistant trees are a marvel of evolution. They are trees that have adapted to withstand the heat and flames of wildfires, making them invaluable in areas affected by this destructive force. These trees have thicker bark, higher moisture content, and can regenerate quickly after fires. Their leaves are typically smaller and more densely packed, reducing their surface area and making them less flammable. This unique combination of traits makes them more resilient to wildfires than other trees, providing a vital resource for communities and ecosystems affected by fires.

One of the key adaptations of fire-resistant trees is their thick bark. This bark protects the tree's core and roots from damage, allowing it to survive even the hottest fires. Additionally, fire-resistant trees often have a deep root system that can access water sources in times of drought, ensuring that they continue to grow even in harsh conditions. And when wildfires do occur, these trees are ready to bounce back. They can quickly regenerate new growth from their roots, ensuring that their species will continue to thrive for generations to come.

Evolutionary reason:

Climate change and land-use practices have had a significant impact on wildfires, which have become more frequent and intense in recent years. As a result, fire-resistant trees have become increasingly important in areas affected by wildfires, as they are better able to withstand the heat and flames of these destructive forces.

Fire-resistant trees have evolved over time to be particularly adept at surviving fires. These trees have a range of adaptations that make them more resilient to wildfires than other trees. For example, they have thicker bark, higher moisture content, smaller and more densely packed leaves, and the ability to regenerate quickly after fires.

As wildfires become more common, these trees will become increasingly important in areas affected by these destructive forces, providing vital ecosystem services and helping to ensure the survival of many different species. By planting fire-resistant trees, we can help to ensure a brighter and more resilient future for ourselves, our communities, and our planet.

III

MICROORGANISMS

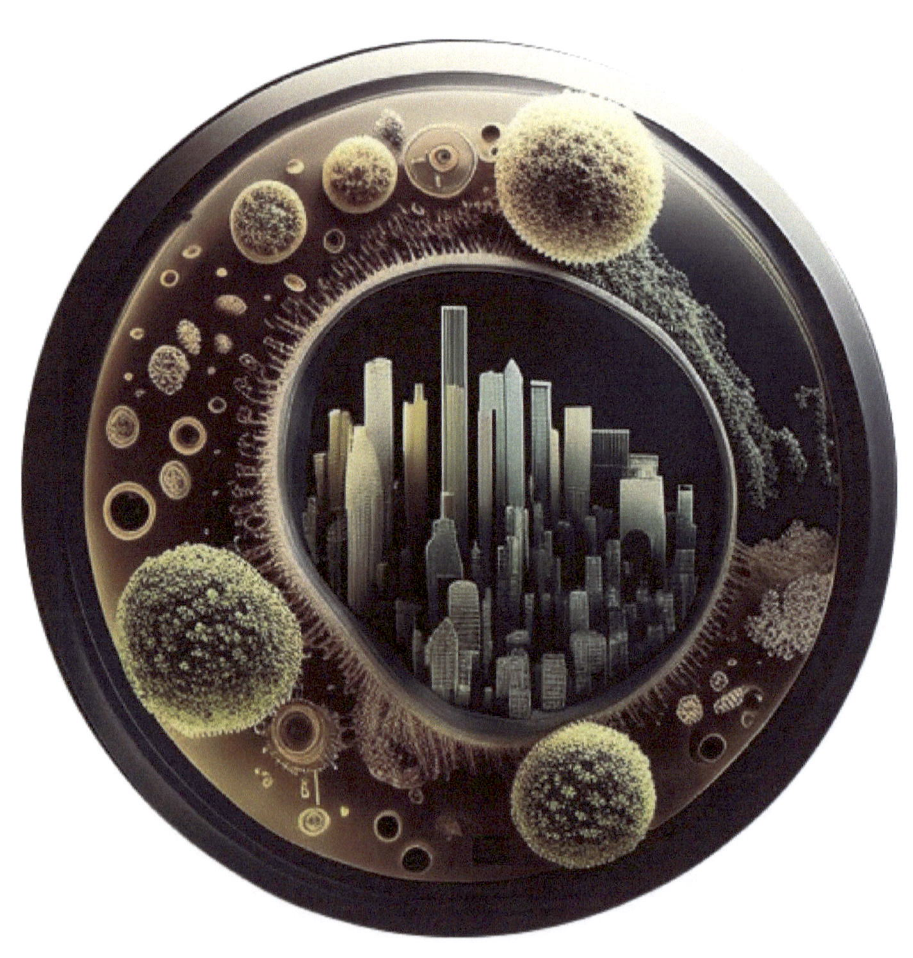

Plastic-Eating Bacteria

Plastic pollution has become one of the biggest environmental problems of our time, and finding ways to combat it has become a top priority for scientists and researchers worldwide. One of the most promising solutions to this problem is the use of plastic-eating bacteria - tiny organisms that have evolved to consume plastic waste.

These bacteria are not only fascinating to study, but they also possess incredible abilities that could revolutionize the way we manage our plastic waste. For instance, scientists are already exploring the possibility of creating custom bacteria that can target specific types of plastics, breaking them down into harmless compounds. This could offer a sustainable, cost-effective solution to one of the biggest environmental problems we face today.

The potential benefits of plastic-eating bacteria don't stop there, either. By studying the enzymes that these bacteria use to break down plastic, scientists could unlock new scientific breakthroughs in the field of biotechnology. They could use this knowledge to develop new, innovative ways to break down other complex materials, such as oil spills and toxic chemicals. This could have a transformative impact on environmental remediation, making it faster, more efficient, and more sustainable.

But how exactly do plastic-eating bacteria work? These tiny organisms possess enzymes that can break down the complex chemical bonds in plastic polymers, allowing them to feed on plastic waste and breaking it down into simpler compounds that can be utilized as a food source. They are also highly efficient and able to adapt to a variety of environments, including highly contaminated areas. This makes them an incredibly powerful tool in the fight against plastic pollution.

Evolutionary reason:

The evolution of plastic-eating bacteria is also a fascinating topic. Researchers believe that these organisms have evolved to feed on plastic waste under the condition of human assistance, breaking down this persistent pollutant in the environment. It's incredible to think that these tiny organisms could have adapted to feed on plastic waste, becoming more efficient and effective over time. With our help, they could be the solution to one of the biggest environmental challenges of our time.

In conclusion, plastic-eating bacteria offer a sustainable, cost-effective solution to one of the biggest environmental problems we face today. By harnessing the natural abilities of these tiny organisms, we can take a big step forward in the fight against plastic pollution and pave the way for a more sustainable future. So let's work together to embrace the power of plastic-eating bacteria and create a cleaner, healthier planet for all of us.

CO2-Fixing Bacteria

CO2-fixing bacteria are fascinating microorganisms that play a critical role in reducing the concentration of carbon dioxide in the atmosphere. By harnessing the power of photosynthesis, these tiny unicellular creatures are able to convert carbon dioxide into organic matter, a process that has significant implications for mitigating the effects of climate change.

But what makes CO2-fixing bacteria so special? For starters, they are incredibly versatile. They can be found in a wide range of habitats, from the soil beneath our feet to the depths of the ocean. They are also able to use a variety of energy sources to fuel their metabolic processes, including sunlight, organic matter, and inorganic compounds.

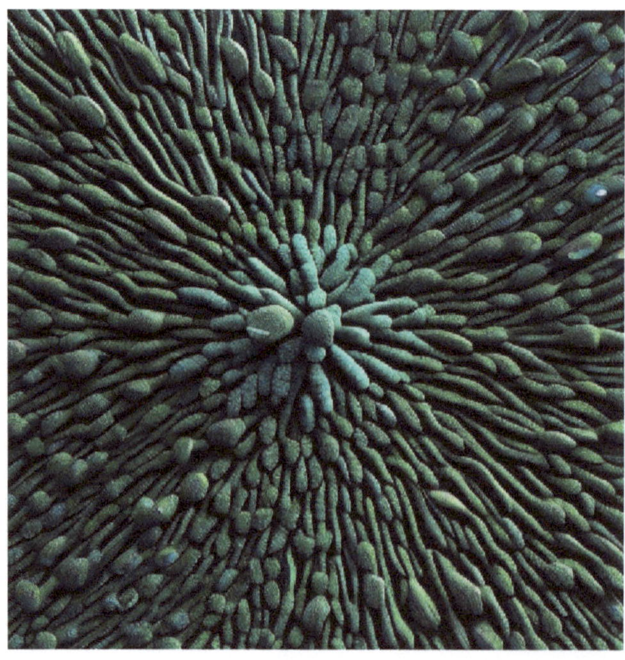

Perhaps most impressive of all, CO2-fixing bacteria are masters of photosynthesis. Using a variety of different pigments, including chlorophyll, bacteriochlorophyll, and carotenoids, these microorganisms are able to capture light energy and convert it into chemical energy, which is then used to synthesize organic molecules from carbon dioxide. And thanks to the complex concave-convex texture of their surface, they have a larger surface area, which allows them to effectively contact and capture external carbon dioxide molecules.

Evolutionary reason:

It's likely that rising levels of carbon dioxide in the atmosphere played a significant role. Bacteria that were able to fix carbon dioxide and convert it into organic matter would have had a distinct advantage in such an environment, allowing them to thrive and evolve into the powerful organisms they are today.

The rise of CO2 in the atmosphere is a result of the burning of fossil fuels, which is a human activity that has been increasing in scale and frequency over the past few centuries. When we burn fossil fuels like coal, oil, and gas to power our homes, cars, and factories, we release large amounts of carbon dioxide into the atmosphere. This carbon dioxide, which was previously trapped underground for millions of years, is now being released at an unprecedented rate, leading to a rapid increase in the concentration of CO2 in the atmosphere.

The rise of CO2 in the atmosphere could have been an "opportunity" for the bacteria to thrive and evolve. As atmospheric carbon dioxide levels rose, bacteria that were able to fix carbon dioxide and convert it into organic matter would have had a distinct advantage. This allowed them to grow and reproduce more efficiently than other bacteria that were unable to fix CO2. Over time, this gave rise to a new group of bacteria that could convert CO2 into organic matter, a process that would have been critical in maintaining the balance of carbon in the Earth's atmosphere. The evolution of CO2-fixing bacteria may have played a crucial role in the long-term regulation of atmospheric carbon dioxide levels and the maintenance of a habitable environment for life on Earth.

Antibiotic-resistant bacteria

Antibiotic-resistant bacteria are a growing threat to human health. They are able to survive exposure to antibiotics and continue to multiply, causing infections that are difficult, and sometimes impossible, to treat. The overuse and misuse of antibiotics in medicine and agriculture has created a perfect breeding ground for antibiotic-resistant bacteria to thrive.

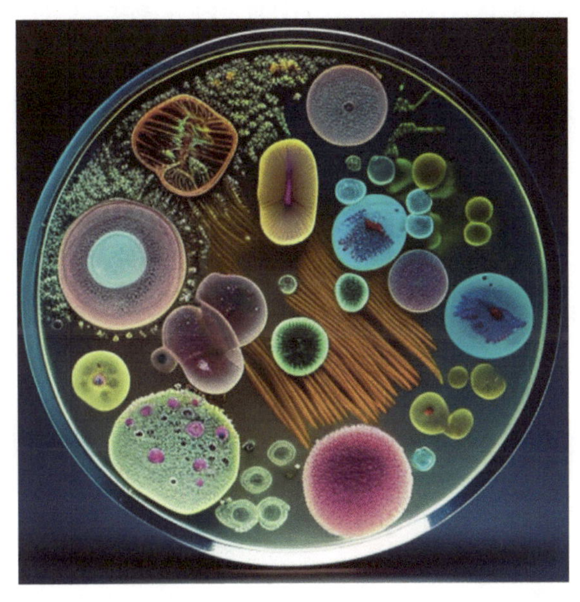

These bacteria possess subtle changes at the molecular level that give them the ability to survive and multiply in the presence of antibiotics. They may have slight variations in their cell wall or outer membrane, which can make them more resistant to the action of antibiotics. They may also have an increased ability to pump out antibiotics that enter the cell, which reduces the concentration of the drug inside the bacteria and makes it less effective.

But the problem is not just a matter of bacteria becoming resistant to antibiotics. It is also about the evolution of bacteria. Antibiotic resistance is not a new phenomenon. It has been around since the first antibiotics were introduced in the 1940s. However, the problem has become more severe in recent years due to the widespread use of antibiotics.

Dealing with antibiotic-resistant bacteria is a complex and ongoing challenge. The development of new antibiotics has slowed down, and the bacteria have become more resistant to the ones that currently exist. This has created a need for alternative treatments, such as phage therapy, which uses viruses to target and kill specific bacteria.

It is important to remember that antibiotics are not a cure-all. They are effective against bacterial infections, but not against viral infections. Overuse and misuse of antibiotics can lead to the development of antibiotic-resistant bacteria, which can pose a serious threat to human health.

Therefore, it is crucial that antibiotics be used correctly and only when they are needed. This means that the correct dose and duration of treatment should be prescribed, and antibiotics should not be used to treat viral infections. We must also explore alternative treatments to antibiotics and invest in research to develop new antibiotics.

In conclusion, antibiotic-resistant bacteria are a serious threat to human health, and it is up to all of us to take action to prevent the development of these dangerous bacteria. By using antibiotics correctly, developing alternative treatments, and investing in research, we can help to ensure that antibiotics remain an effective tool against bacterial infections for years to come.

Evolutionary reason:

People tend to overuse antibiotics for several reasons. One of the main reasons is a misunderstanding of how antibiotics work. Many people believe that antibiotics are effective against all types of infections, including viral infections, which is not true. Another reason is the pressure from patients to receive antibiotics, even when they are not necessary. Additionally, some doctors may prescribe antibiotics as a precautionary measure, even if the infection is not caused by bacteria. Finally, the availability of antibiotics without a prescription in some countries can also contribute to their overuse.

The overuse of antibiotics in medicine and agriculture has put selective pressure on bacteria to evolve resistance to these drugs. Bacteria that can survive in the presence of antibiotics can outcompete their non-resistant counterparts, leading to the evolution of antibiotic-resistant strains.

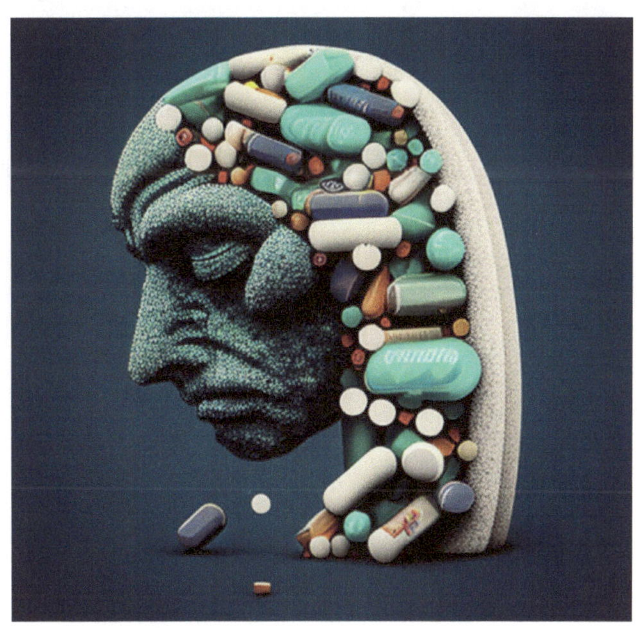

Magnetotactic bacteria

Magnetotactic bacteria are a fascinating group of microorganisms that have evolved to sense and move along magnetic fields. These tiny creatures are found in aquatic environments and can be identified under a microscope as small, rod-shaped or spiral-shaped cells with tiny magnetic particles inside.

The ability to sense and move along magnetic fields provides magnetotactic bacteria with a selective advantage in certain environments. By locating areas with optimal conditions for growth and survival, such as areas with high oxygen levels or specific chemical gradients, these bacteria are able to thrive and reproduce. Over time, magnetotactic bacteria have developed different strategies for controlling their movement along the magnetic field lines, allowing them to navigate effectively and efficiently.

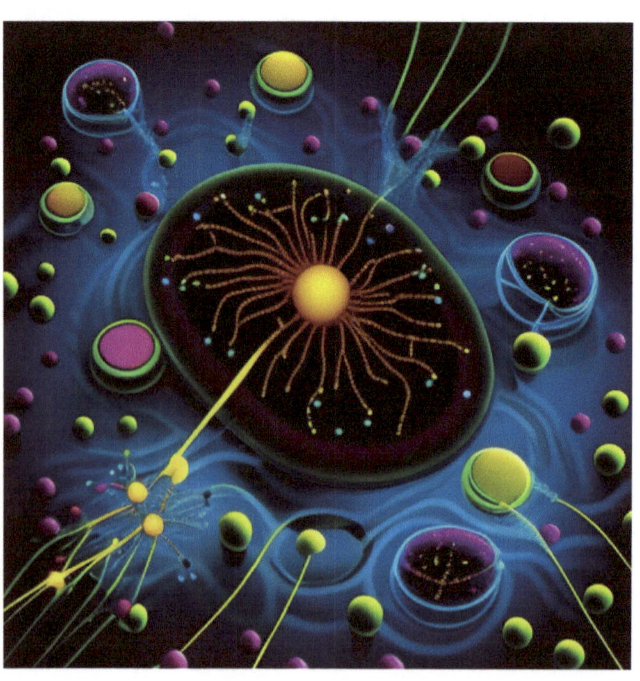

In addition to their unique sensory abilities, magnetotactic bacteria also have a fascinating diet. They can be chemoautotrophic, meaning they derive energy from the oxidation of inorganic chemicals such as iron or sulfur. This metabolic flexibility allows these bacteria to thrive in a variety of environments, from deep sea hydrothermal vents to freshwater streams.

The study of magnetotactic bacteria has important implications for a variety of fields, from microbiology to materials science. By understanding the mechanisms behind their magnetic sensing and navigation, researchers may be able to develop new technologies for environmental monitoring, biomedical imaging, and more.

Overall, magnetotactic bacteria are a remarkable example of the complexity and diversity of life on Earth. Their evolution and adaptation to their environment provide important insights into the workings of the natural world, and their unique abilities may hold the key to solving a variety of scientific and technological challenges in the future

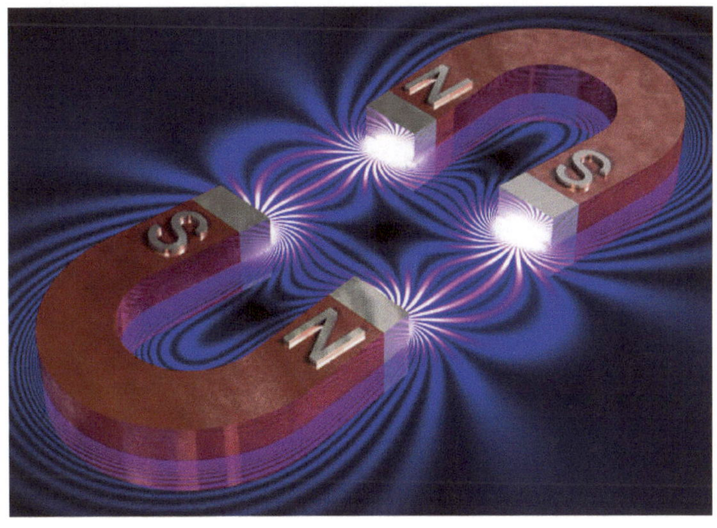

Evolutionary reason:

But what is the evolutionary reason behind magnetotactic bacteria? The answer lies in the selective pressure of the environment. In the aquatic environment, the existence of magnetic minerals provides a clue for bacteria to locate and move to the area where they eat magnetic food. For these microorganisms, the ability to sense and navigate along the magnetic field is beneficial, which enables them to find a favorable environment for survival and growth.

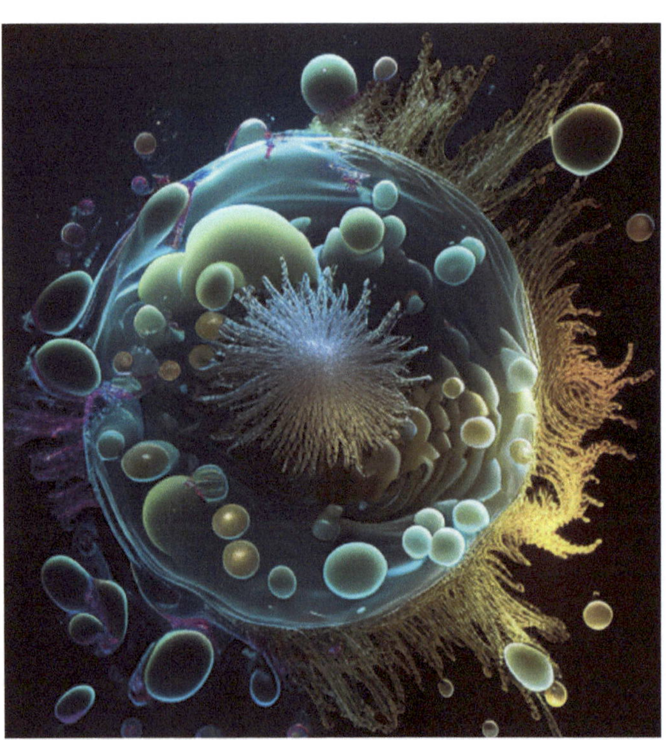

Metal-Metabolizing Bacteria

Metal-metabolizing bacteria are some of the most fascinating and unique organisms on the planet. These tiny creatures have the remarkable ability to consume and metabolize metals, a feat that was once thought impossible. So how did these incredible bacteria evolve to thrive in such harsh and toxic environments?

The answer lies in their unique features. Metal-metabolizing bacteria have developed several adaptations that allow them to survive in metal-rich environments. One of the most impressive adaptations is their ability to transfer electrons from the interior of the cell to the exterior, interacting with metals in their environment. This process, known as extracellular electron transfer, is essential for their survival.

But metal-metabolizing bacteria aren't just capable of interacting with metals - they can also oxidize them to make them more accessible for consumption. This process is crucial for their survival in metal-rich environments, where other organisms would struggle to survive.

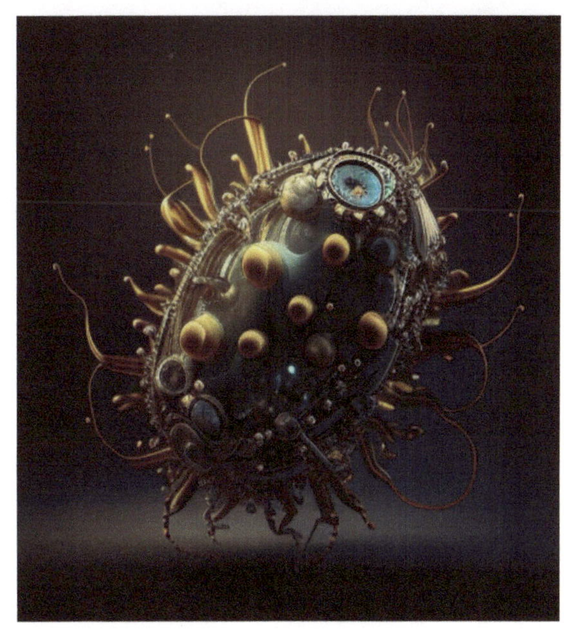

One of the most interesting adaptations of metal-metabolizing bacteria is their unique energy metabolism. These bacteria can use the energy from metal oxidation to generate ATP, the energy currency of cells. This unique ability allows them to thrive in environments where other organisms cannot survive.

Overall, metal-metabolizing bacteria are a testament to the incredible adaptability of life on Earth. These tiny creatures have evolved to thrive in even the harshest and most toxic environments.

Although it may be beneficial for the treatment of metal contaminants, this poses new problems for future metal corrosion protection. While people are considering traditional anti-rust methods for metal instruments, they may also need to consider how to sterilize them.

Revolutionary reason:

The evolution of metal-metabolizing bacteria can be attributed to the need to survive in metal-rich environments. As some bacteria adapted to these environments, they developed the unique features that allowed them to consume and metabolize metals. Over time, these traits were passed down to subsequent generations, leading to the evolution of metal-metabolizing bacteria.

But why do these bacteria need to adapt to metal-rich environments in the first place? The answer lies in the natural occurrence of heavy metals in the environment. Heavy metals such as lead, mercury, and cadmium are naturally present in rocks and soil, and can also be released into the environment through human activities such as mining, industrial waste disposal, and agricultural practices.

As a result, metal-metabolizing bacteria have had to adapt to survive in these harsh environments. Through natural selection, the bacteria that possess genes that provide resistance to toxic metals are better equipped to survive and reproduce, passing on their resistance to their offspring. Over time, this has led to the evolution of metal-metabolizing bacteria that are highly specialized to thrive in metal-rich environments.

Photosynthetic Fungi

Photosynthetic fungi are a truly remarkable group of organisms that are revolutionizing our understanding of the world around us. These fascinating fungi have the unique ability to harness the power of the sun and convert it into energy, just like plants. This ability has allowed them to thrive in environments where other fungi cannot survive, giving them a competitive edge in the world of natural selection.

One of the most intriguing aspects of photosynthetic fungi is their ability to form symbiotic relationships with other organisms. Some species of photosynthetic fungi form mutualistic relationships with plants, providing them with essential nutrients while also benefiting from the plant's waste products. This remarkable cooperation between two very different organisms is a testament to the power of nature and the importance of diversity in the natural world.

But photosynthetic fungi are not just passive players in the ecosystem. They are active participants in the breakdown of dead plant material, releasing nutrients back into the soil and helping to support the growth of new plants. This crucial role in the nutrient cycle is one of the many ways in which these fungi contribute to the health of our planet.

In conclusion, photosynthetic fungi are a vital and fascinating group of organisms that have so much to teach us about the world around us. From their unique ability to harness the power of the sun to their complex relationships with other organisms, these fungi are truly one of nature's wonders.

Evolutionary reason:

Photosynthetic fungi have evolved to perform photosynthesis, which is the process of converting sunlight into energy. This process is typically performed by higher green plants. Through the process of natural selection, some Mutant fungi obtaining the ability to perform photosynthesis were more likely to survive and reproduce in environments with limited resources. Over time, these fungi evolved to become more efficient at photosynthesis and developed specialized structures, such as pigments and chloroplasts, to help capture and use sunlight.

New virus

Not only could viruses be the simplest organisms, but easiest to evolve, so it is difficult to predict exactly which new viruses will appear in the future, but there are some factors that may contribute to their emergence. One of the most significant factors is the increasing population density and globalization, which creates more opportunities for viruses to spread and mutate. Climate change and environmental destruction can also lead to the emergence of new viruses by disrupting ecosystems and causing species to move into new areas.

Moreover, the ever-evolving nature of viruses and their ability to mutate quickly means that new strains are constantly emerging. Human activities, such as intensive agriculture and deforestation, can also increase the likelihood of viruses jumping from animals to humans, as well as allowing existing viruses to spread more easily.

Additionally, the increasing use of antibiotics and antiviral drugs can lead to the development of drug-resistant strains of viruses, making them more difficult to treat and control. Finally, bioterrorism and the accidental release of dangerous viruses from laboratories are also potential sources of new viral threats in the future.

Here, based on our understanding of modern human science and social development, we can logically hypothesize several new viruses that may appear in the future and are difficult to deal with.

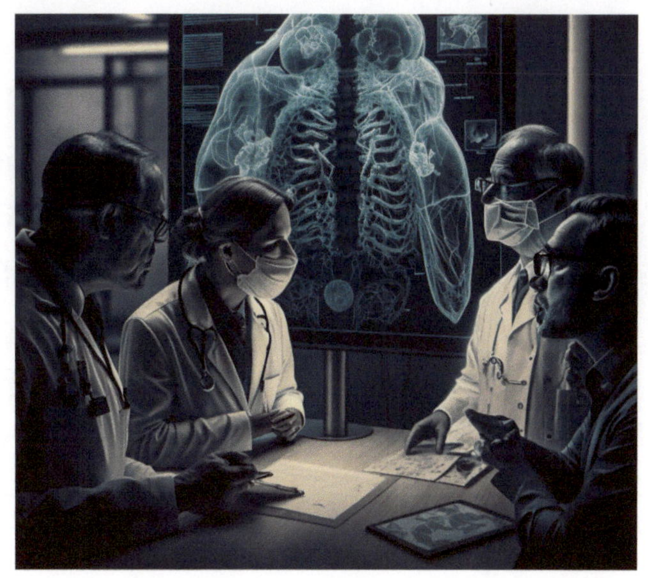

- Nano-virus: A virus is small, so that it can penetrate cell membranes and evade the immune system. It would likely have a simple structure, with a single strand of RNA or DNA wrapped in a protein shell. Under a microscope, it appears as a small, non-enveloped virus with a diameter of approximately only 20 nanometers. The virus has a characteristic icosahedral shape and a symmetrical structure with triangular faces.
- Vaccine-resistant virus: This virus mutates rapidly, making it difficult to develop effective vaccines. It would likely have a complex structure with many surface proteins that can quickly change in response to selective pressure; Or Just like the known AIDS virus, this virus attacks the immune system specifically, thus making the traditional vaccine ineffective.
- Chimeric virus: A virus that is created by combining genetic material from multiple viral strains, potentially resulting in a highly infectious and virulent pathogen. It would likely have a mixed structure with features from each of the parent viruses.

The global pandemic brought about by the new coronavirus, also known as COVID-19, has brought significant enlightenment to humanity. The pandemic has caused an unprecedented loss of human life, disrupted economies and livelihoods, and caused serious social problems and permanent stress. It has also exposed the weaknesses and strengths of global health systems, increased the awareness of the importance of public health measures, and spurred the development of vaccines and treatments at an unprecedented pace.

One of the most significant lessons that the pandemic has taught us is the importance of preparedness for infectious disease outbreaks. The pandemic has highlighted the need for robust and resilient public health systems capable of detecting, responding, and controlling disease outbreaks effectively and quickly. has also revealed the importance of timely and accurate information sharing, transparency, and international cooperation in responding to global health emergencies.

There are several traditional measures that can be taken to prevent the large-scale spread of viruses:

- Vaccinations: Vaccinations are the most effective way to prevent the spread of viruses. By vaccinating a large percentage of the population, we can create herd immunity, which means that the virus will have difficulty spreading within the population.
- Contact tracing: Contact tracing involves identifying and tracking the contacts of infected individuals. This allows for quick identification and isolation of potentially infected individuals, preventing further spread of the virus.
- Social distancing: Social distancing measures such as wearing masks, avoiding large gatherings, and maintaining physical distance can prevent the spread of viruses by limiting close contact between individuals.
- Improved hygiene practices: Good hygiene practices such as frequent hand washing and sanitizing can prevent the spread of viruses by reducing the transmission of the virus from contaminated surfaces to individuals.

- Early detection and treatment: Early detection and treatment of infected individuals can prevent the spread of the virus by isolating and treating infected individuals before they have a chance to spread the virus to others.

Last but not least, a sound social system achieves balance among various interest groups through decentralization and checks and balances. This fosters open and transparent virus research, as any issues in any link can be reported in a timely and sufficient manner in public, and misconduct will be held accountable, which significantly increases the cost of wrongdoing. These measures promote virus research that benefits humankind. However, under a flawed social system, the media may only serve as a tool for propaganda to help cover up the truth. Opaque information can easily be manipulated by a few individuals, who may use virus research as a means to achieve their political goals by developing biological and chemical weapons, ultimately endangering human society.

Postscript

As we continue to learn more about the impact of human development on the environment, it's important to remember that we all have a role to play in creating a sustainable future. This book introduces young readers to the fascinating world of evolutionary biology and encourages them to think about the impact of their actions on the planet.

All the creatures in the illustrations in this book are generated by AI and do not exist in reality to increase the interest and vividness of this book. But this does not affect this book as a good popular science book for children and teenagers, because the logic of predicting future creatures is based on contemporary evolution theory, as well as scientific predictions of human activities on the current ecological environment and climate change. As with the logic behind the famous case of the black peppered moth (Appendix A), human impact on the environment and on biological evolution is undeniable. Moreover, the case is only the impact on species change in a few decades

We hope that this book will inspire readers to become more mindful of the environment and to take action to protect the planet. Whether it's through reducing our carbon footprint, supporting environmental organizations, or simply learning more about the world around us, we can all make a difference.

Thank you for taking this journey of discovery with us, and we hope that this book will spark your curiosity and inspire you to become a steward of the environment.

Appendix A

The Peppered Moth is a widespread species in Britain and Ireland and is frequently found in ordinary back gardens. However, its amazing story has made it famous all over the world as one of the best-known examples of evolution by natural selection, which was Darwin's great discovery. It is often referred to as "Darwin's moth".

Peppered Moths are normally white with black speckles across the wings, which give them their name. This patterning makes them well camouflaged against lichen-covered tree trunks when they rest on them during the day.

There is also a naturally occurring genetic mutation that causes some moths to have almost black wings. These black forms, called "melanic", are not as well camouflaged as normal "peppered" forms against lichens, and are more likely to be eaten by birds and other predators. As a result, fewer black forms survive to breed, so they are less common in the population than the paler peppered forms. This is the normal situation observed in the countryside of Britain and Ireland.

However, in the 19th century, it was noticed that in towns and cities, it was actually the black form of the moth that was more common than the pale peppered form. Industrialization and domestic coal fires had caused sooty air pollution, which had killed off lichens and blackened urban tree trunks and walls. This made the pale form of the moth more obvious to predators, while the melanic form was better camouflaged and more likely to survive and produce offspring. As a result, over successive generations, the black moths came to outnumber the pale forms in urban areas.

Since moths are short-lived, this evolution by natural selection happened quite quickly. For example, the first black Peppered Moth was recorded in Manchester in 1848, and by 1895, 98% of Peppered Moths in the city were black.

In the mid-20th century, controls were introduced to reduce air pollution, and as the air quality improved, tree trunks became cleaner and lichen growth increased. Once again, the normal pale Peppered Moths were camouflaged, and the black forms were more noticeable. Now the situation in urban areas has again become the same as in the countryside, with normal pale Peppered Moths being far more common than the black forms. So, natural selection has been seen to work in both directions, always favoring the moth that is best suited to the environmental conditions. The same thing has been observed throughout Europe and the USA.